Maine Girl
Poetry by Deborah McGlauflin

> "Should fate unkind send us to roam
> The scent of the fragrant pines,
> The tang of the salty sea will call us home."
>
> From the *State of Maine Song*
> Written and Composed by Roger Vinton Snow

Cover Photo credit: © Richard Gunion | Dreamstime.com
Cover design assistance from Jocie Salveson

Copyright 2011 Deborah McGlauflin. All rights reserved, including the right of reproduction in whole or in part in any form.

Library of Congress Cataloging-in-Publication Data
McGlauflin, Deborah
McGlauflin, Debbi
Maine Girl

ISBN 978-1-105-05764-9

Contents

Remembering the Pines	5
Loon Tune	7
Deep Winter on the Farm	9
Forty Mile Woods	11
Fiddleheads	13
Memory of Moose	15
First Lobster	17
Potato Picking	19
The Duchess of No Trout	21
Something to Yack About	23
Catfish	25
In Praise of Maples	27
Canoe Lesson	29
Yonder	31
Grounded	33

Dedication
About the Author

Remembering the Pines

Memory treads the needled bed under cathedral pines
How towering deep the pillowed hush
Latticed boughs mincing sunlight
Into dusty biblical shafts
Decades later this wandering Maine girl still pauses
Faint linger of pinecone pitch on wrinkling hands
Recalling the evergreen promise of profound eternity

© Jason Kasumovic | Dreamstime.com

Loon Tune

Trilling weave of birdcall and moonlight
Glides on shivered lake to my shore
Arresting thought of who and where
I am
Solitary together at peace
No after, no before

Deep Winter on the Farm

Always only and forever snow,
    no memory or possibility of Spring
Pitiless piling of moisture by wind and man
    Arctic howl bites bone and blood shivers
Bluing digits numbed by mercury's tumble

Relentless white punctuated only by
    skeleton snow fences and red flags on car antennas
Signaling danger to bundled schoolkids
    Pounding mittens to keep warm as they wait for the bus
Behind muffling mountains left by giant plows

Icicles of sounds frozen in memory:
    shrieking sled down the roof of the potato barn,
Scraping through to the ice on the pond,
    skating on raspy double-edged blades,
Boots' crunch in the crystalline night

Dad returns home after a big storm
    from high atop a towering snowbank
I watch as my parents dig blind to meet
    directing, "More to the left, Mom!
Hey, I think I can see Spring from up here!"

© Timothy Epp | Dreamstime.com

Forty Mile Woods

The Hainesville Woods from the interstate
Hide olde deep and dark ways
But I see their truth
Forty miles of back-road hills and turns
Sorrow etched in ice each milepost
Two I know too well
The one at Santa Claus Hill
Where my uncle's truck brakes
Failed and left him lifelong lame
And the one where my grandparents died
Tearful childhood Christmas Eve
Our family's toll a wreck beneath hushed pines
Remembered passing

© Monsteranimal | Dreamstime.com

Fiddleheads

Succulent buds spring fresh from waking earth
Coiled tight and furry sweatered 'gainst night's chill
Muted gray green promise at long winter's end
That summer too will unfurl beneath unbooted feet
It's time for Maine folk, shivering ostriches of the North,
To lift their heads from the snow and stretch up smiling
To bask in the fleeting warmth of longer days

© Paul Binet | Dreamstime.com

Memory of Moose

Mostly memory of moose is myth
Stories told by summer bonfires of
Antlered menace's bellowing charge
Tall tales about the huge stuffed head
Above the Y camp's rocky hearth

But one memory of moose is mine and true
From girlhood's past unfaded
While trolling from a boat midstream
Drifting through the peaceful pines
A single shot cracked loud and lethal

Off from the right dense forest bank
Came anguished howl of giant's pain
Then answering close by on the left
A bull moose tore through tangled brush
Majestic grace in headlong motion

His fearless ford to mate and fate
We witnessed awestruck frozen
The splendor in our wake receded
Until a final hail of shots mortified
Confounding remembrance still

© Mikael Damkier | Dreamstime.com

First Lobster

At six I knew what I wanted
My very own lobster to eat
No mere claw from Mom's
Expensive child my father groaned
But smiling at the inevitable

Any Maine Girl worth her seasalt
Wouldn't want an ounce less
Than one pound boiled red
Buttered within sight of surf
Perfumed with tideborne kelp

Seagulls shrieked yes
A ferry horn salute
Proud he said sure

© Reino Jonsson | Dreamstime.com

Potato Picking

No new clothes for school's start back then
Not long we knew until the three week break
When every able hand soft or calloused
Headed to the fields racing the first snow
To pick potatoes, baskets to barrels, dawn to dusk

Back-breaking work but honest beside migrant workers
A quarter a barrel added up sorely but proudly
To shiny shoes and warm gloves and sweaters
Farmer's wives in roadside stands sprouted overnight
Selling new potatoes with friendly smiles

Then hard times' harvest of auction signs
Tired old farmers got done, few took their place
Too rough a row to hoe youth would say when leaving
Many to return each July for a festival of memories
Amidst Aroostook blossoms' aching beauty

© Gergo Orban | Dreamstime.com

The Duchess of No Trout

Duchess would wade in summer streams
Amidst darting trout of no consequence
Her concern instead with animals come to drink
Faint proof in scents and prints along the muddy banks
Alert she'd splash to every rustle in the brush
The endless joy of maybe a moose!

When Dad had put on his waders, when he'd read
The pools and eddies and chosen the right fly
Time would come for dog's play to cease
A whistle and one slap on his left leg
Out on the left bank and quiet she would lie
In swaying shafts of sifted sunlight

Later, cold enough and with trout to cook (or not)
Two slaps OK to frolic before heading home
Rising slowly with a long contented stretch
Enough a quenching drink at stream's edge
Furry reflection shimmering in the shallows
Illusive trout swimming in dog's dewy eyes

Something to Yack About

Strange horse, curiously partial to engines
Ears perked to every distant car's call
One window for its coming, one for its going
Tireless tally from his corner stall

One frigid winter morn, windows laced with ice
Pat, hearing but not seeing, was fazed
Stuck his head through one pane then two
Cut and bloodied his determined gaze

Repairs lasted only 'til the next hoary frost
Uncle Homer shrugged leaving stubborn horse his view
From the coldest stall out on the State Road
Gave the neighbors something to yack about too

Not just cars Pat fancied but some appliances
My mom found out one bright spring day
Vacuuming with the windows wide open
When Pat came calling in his nosey way
A good laugh *that* got in Mapleton

© Michael Mill | Dreamstime.com

Catfish

Shudder the catfish, deeply anchored
Nemesis of childhood fishing trips
On Eagle Lake and otherwheres
Always first they were to take my bait
Sluggish tug on the line and I'd know
I'd caught another whiskered fiend

"Get your line off bottom," Dad would say
I'd surely try but they seemed to know
This little girl was a reel cat person
They'd take turns over the gunwhale
Gasping grayly in the bottom of the boat
Them out of water, me out of sorts

Their luck, we had a deal, Dad and I
He'd free each wretch from my hook
And toss them back with "Try again."
Another worm and cast, another chance
Daydreaming dogfish and micefish
Going home happy with even a perch

© Robertplotz | Dreamstime.com

In Praise of Maples

Canada close and clearly wise
Its flag with noble leaf
Proof enough to this child's eyes
No need for more belief

The welcome flight of whirlybirds
Playful summery delights
Descend in softly spinning herds
How teasingly they light

Soon fiery colors warm the chill
Of autumn's darkening day
Then lay a carpet purposeful
To decorate the way

But best of all the sap that brings
At winter's end sweet gift
A sugar shock to lagging spring
A promise coming swift

Across treed border rich and poor
Lift up voices now and gazes
In thanks for all these gifts and more
Join in singing maple's praises

© Yanik Chauvin | Dreamstime.com

Canoe Lesson

No sense there is to a canoe seat
Surest way to tip and dip in an ice cold lake
Comfort's lofty tease soon tells the lie
Aloofness spurned, left sputtering

But venture down on tender knees hips low
The foregone seat mere incidental brace
With water lapping close, dip paddle gently
Then, caressed and caressing, flow as one

© Kwerry | Dreamstime.com

Yonder

Seaplane rising through the morning mist
Loons scattering briefly in its wake
Gliding back to their familiar dives
Choosing to remain and not to follow

This child that day chose differently
In daydream taking eager wing
Past roads' end to uncommon lakes
Glimpsing the serenely seldom seen

Grounded

To have Maine in one's blood
Is to know well the love of place
To feel the heart's tie with what lies
Noticed underfoot, to live apace

The gift of Maine seen from afar
Is that this love of place conveys
Rooted even in the uprooted
Wherever they wend their ways

No separation in the distance
Just look down and see the fact
Every curve of earth traces surely
Back to the state's compelling tract

So know Maine to be close at hand
No matter where you roam
To honor the ground on which you stand
Is your instant passport home

Dedication

Dedicated with love to Mom and Dad,
Who gave me wings and taught me
To trust that, though I might leave Maine,
It would never leave me.

About the Author

Maine Girl Deborah (Debbi) McGlauflin
now lives happily by the Chesapeake Bay
She has published two other poetry collections: *Lucky Enough!* and *Getting Over Me*.

Her poetry can be found online at:
http://mainegirl.net

www.ingramcontent.com/pod-product-compliance
Lightning Source LLC
Chambersburg PA
CBHW040925190426
43197CB00032B/38